Train Your Brain

Strengthen Your Vocabulary and Spelling Skills

Published in 2023 by Windmill Books, an Imprint of Rosen Publishing
29 East 21st Street, New York, NY 10010

Copyright © 2020 Editorial Sol90, S.L. Barcelona
All rights reserved.

No part of this book may be reproduced in any form without permission in writing from the publisher, except by a reviewer.

Cataloging-in-Publication Data

Names: Navarro, Àngels.
Title: Strengthen your vocabulary and spelling skills / Àngels Navarro.
Description: New York : Windmill Publishing, 2023. | Series: Train your brain
Identifiers: ISBN 9781499489965 (pbk.) | ISBN 9781499489989 (library bound) | ISBN 9781499489972 (6pack) | ISBN 9781499489996 (ebook)
Subjects: LCSH: English language--Orthography and spelling--Juvenile literature. | Vocabulary--Juvenile literature.
Classification: LCC PE1145.2 N377 2023 | DDC 428.1--dc23

Idea and overall concept: Nuria Cicero
Coordination: Emilio López
Design: Claudia Andrade, Laura Ocampo, Irene Morales, Àngels Rambla i Vidal
Design adaptation: Raúl Rodriguez, R studiot T, NYC
Editor: Diana Osorio
Editors and proofreaders: Alberto Hernández, Marta Kordon, Diana Malizia, Joan Soriano
Games and content:
Àngels Navarro y encargos puntuales de La Usina, energía creativa, SRL
Editorial production: Montse Martínez

Manufactured in the United States of America

CPSIA Compliance Information: Batch #CSWM23. For Further Information contact Rosen Publishing, New York, New York at 1-800-237-9932.

Contents

Introduction 3
Activities 4–23
Answer Key 24

Introduction

The puzzles in this book will exercise many different skills you need to succeed in school and in life beyond school. These include logic, reasoning, computation, deduction, vocabulary, memory, and spelling. These puzzles will help you build on your strengths and boost skills that need improvement. Plus they're a lot of fun to do!

Note to Readers

If you have borrowed this book from a school or classroom library, please respect other students and **DO NOT write your answers in the book**. Always write your answers on a separate sheet of paper.

Remember to write your answers on a separate sheet of paper!

1 Words with "Pet"

Complete the words by guiding yourself with the hints.

1. _ _ _ _ P E T (Woven fabric used to cover floors).

2. P E T _ _ _ _ _ _ (Black, oily liquid that is used as fuel or is turned into gasoline).

3. _ _ _ _ P E T (Type of doll that represents a human or an animal, and is moved around with hands, rods, or threads).

4. _ _ _ _ _ P E T (Bronze wind instrument that has a curved tube and a wide bell on one of the ends).

5. P E T _ _ _ _ (A type of plant that has a funnel-shaped flower.)

ON YOUR MARK, GET SET, GO...!

DIFFICULTY:

EASY
MEDIUM
HARD

2 Fifteen on the Line ○

Start off with the 1 located on the top. Keep on going downward as you perform the indicated mathematical operations until you reach the bottom. You need to find the highest possible number.

3 Inheritance ○

A mother leaves an area of land as inheritance to her four daughters. There are 8 trees on the land. How can the four daughters divide the land equally, so that each one of them has two trees on their part of the land? Hint: the four terrains must have the same L shape.

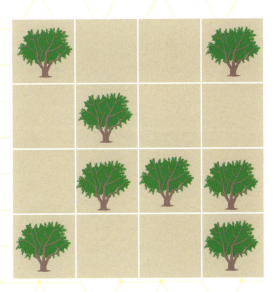

Remember to write your answers on a separate sheet of paper!

4. Pathway ⬤

Can you complete the geometric shapes challenge below? You have to draw a pathway that joins each pair equally. Before starting, you must keep in mind that:

> The pathways can't cross or touch one another.

> Only one pathway can cross through each box.

> Each pathway can be formed by vertical and horizontal moves, but never diagonal!

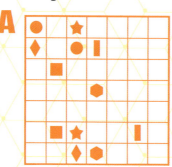

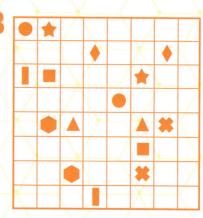

5. Doesn't Belong ⬤

Which of the acrobatic pairs doesn't match the rest? Turn the book around if you need to.

ON YOUR MARK, GET SET, GO...!

DIFFICULTY
EASY ⬤
MEDIUM ⬤
HARD ⬤

6 Domino

The domino game has 28 pieces. Here are 27.
Which one is missing?

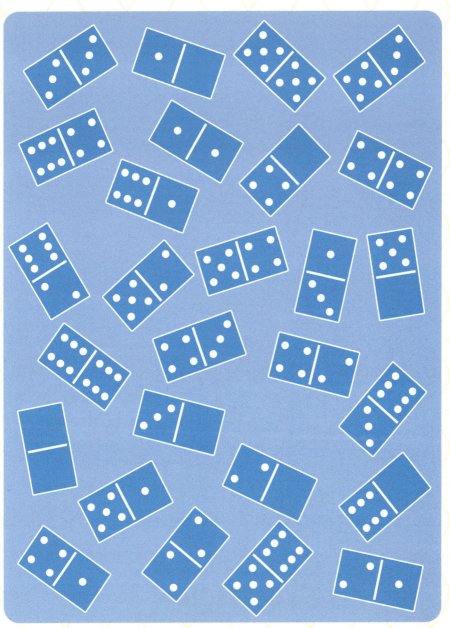

Remember to write your answers on a separate sheet of paper!

7 Trouble at the Farm

A strong wind has caused trouble at the farm. Can you give the farmer a hand? How many of each animal do you see?

ON YOUR MARK, GET SET, GO...!

DIFFICULTY:
EASY
MEDIUM
HARD

8 The Key

Could you help find the key that opens this lock? Check out the possibilities shown below.

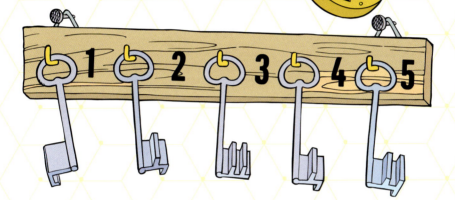

9 Alphabet Riddle

IMPROVE YOUR ENGLISH!

Substitute each letter with the letter that it is followed by in the alphabet to find out what the famous quote says. There's one tricky letter that goes back to the beginning of the alphabet!

HE XNT VZMS RNLDSGHMF CNMD QHFGS, CN HS XNTQRDKE.

Remember to write your answers on a separate sheet of paper!

10 In Search of...

Can you finish this maze? Give it a try!

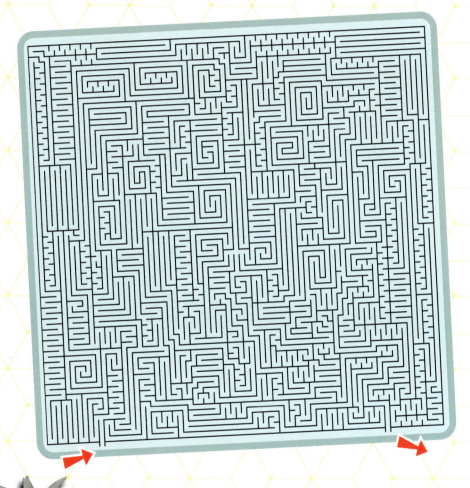

ON YOUR MARK, GET SET, GO...!

DIFFICULTY:

EASY
MEDIUM
HARD

11 The Grove

How many trees can you see here?

12 Girls' Names

Re-order the letters in each word to form five girls' names.

1. LLCEEHIM = _ _ _ _ _ _ _ _
2. ENKITAHRE = _ _ _ _ _ _ _ _ _
3. YRTAC = _ _ _ _ _
4. AMYR = _ _ _ _
5. YWDEN = _ _ _ _ _

Remember to write your answers on a separate sheet of paper!

13 Weight

One brick weighs 6 pounds more than half a brick. How much does a brick and a half weigh?

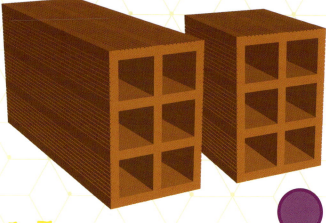

14 Distribution

Distribute the numbers from 1 to 9 so that the numbers inside add up to the three numbers that surround them. To help you, the 6 and the 7 are already placed. Where do the rest go?

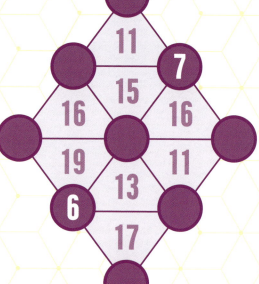

ON YOUR MARK, GET SET, GO...!

DIFFICULTY:
EASY
MEDIUM
HARD

15
Not Like the Others

All these items have something in common, except for one. Find the one that doesn't belong.

Remember to write your answers on a separate sheet of paper!

16 What Letter Comes Next?

What letter should go after 4? A, C, or F?

1 O 2 T 3 T 4 ...

17 More Vocabulary!

Complete this tower with the words that correspond to the following definitions:

1. Animal that meows
2. Vehicle that transports heavy goods
3. Building where there are a lot of books
4. Big stadium or building made for shows. There was one in ancient Rome.

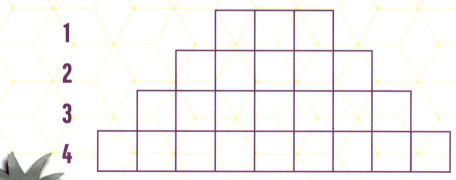

ON YOUR MARK, GET SET, GO...!

DIFFICULTY:
EASY
MEDIUM
HARD

18 Let's Remember!

For a minute, memorize the following instruments. Then, without looking, answer the questions at the bottom of the page.

- CYMBAL
- PIANO
- SAXOPHONE
- TRUMPET
- FLUTE
- BASS
- GUITAR
- ACCORDION
- CLARINET
- DRUM

1. Which are stringed instruments?
2. Which are wind instruments?
3. How many instruments are there in total?

Remember to write your answers on a separate sheet of paper!

IMPROVE YOUR ENGLISH!

19 Feelings Soup

Find 15 words that are hidden below. They are different feelings. Remember that they could be placed diagonally or even backwards.

A	A	P	P	T	A	E	T	A	H	A	T	W	S	S	C	W	P	S
Y	Z	P	S	T	A	X	O	P	K	M	D	A	D	E	I	P	S	H
H	T	E	R	I	L	O	L	O	N	E	L	I	N	E	S	S	O	T
T	F	C	T	C	M	J	A	N	P	L	C	O	N	G	O	J	A	S
A	G	O	G	S	V	C	O	U	R	A	G	E	M	U	P	A	I	N
P	H	N	B	R	I	E	A	A	T	N	S	A	A	O	W	E	A	T
M	K	T	O	R	I	R	G	T	M	C	U	I	I	R	S	U	A	C
Y	B	M	T	A	O	E	T	L	I	H	M	L	O	V	E	I	L	E
S	S	E	N	D	A	S	F	T	D	O	K	A	I	N	L	Ñ	R	F
W	P	D	I	O	C	O	N	D	H	L	T	M	R	O	C	T	E	A
M	A	S	N	O	S	H	A	J	O	Y	M	O	C	D	T	C	G	D
A	S	A	E	R	F	S	Z	I	R	A	L	N	D	N	A	N	N	P
S	S	E	N	R	E	D	N	E	T	O	A	Y	K	L	T	C	A	Z
Q	I	R	S	Z	O	S	Z	C	D	L	C	A	D	Ñ	T	Y	S	X
V	O	U	D	U	P	J	Y	T	E	I	P	I	E	T	R	G	H	C
G	N	B	Z	I	R	T	O	M	R	T	Q	X	D	Z	A	E	R	F

LOVE   LONELINESS   PAIN
GRIEF   NOSTALGIA   PIETY
JOY   MELANCHOLY   SYMPATHY
PAIN   HATE   TENDERNESS
ANGER   PASSION   SADNESS
                               COURAGE

ON YOUR MARK, GET SET, GO...!

DIFFICULTY:
EASY
MEDIUM
HARD

20 Planetary Sudoku

Figure out which symbols belong in the blank boxes. In each row (horizontal) and column (vertical) there must be different symbols. Make sure that they are the correct shape and color. Go for it!

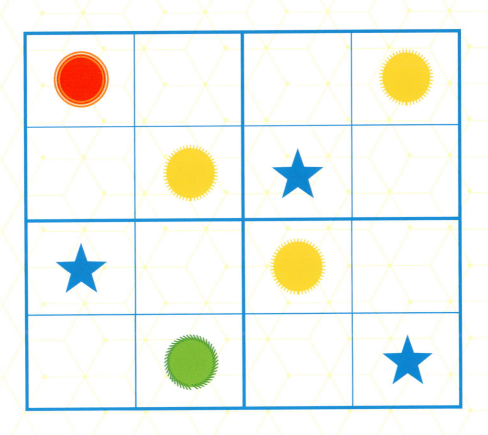

Remember to write your answers on a separate sheet of paper!

21 Crazy Maze

Try to cross through this crazy maze without running into a dead end. How many tries do you think you will need?

ON YOUR MARK, GET SET, GO...!

DIFFICULTY:
EASY
MEDIUM
HARD

22 Continuing the Sequence

Take a look at the sequence below. What do you think are the three pictures that should continue the sequence in the top row?

23 Movie Place

Match the initial of each one of these drawings to the corresponding box to see which word appears. Here's a hint: It is the most famous place in the history of film.

IMPROVE YOUR ENGLISH!

Remember to write your answers on a separate sheet of paper!

24 Inside the Baskets

A farmer went to the market and placed one animal in each basket, but now he can't remember where he placed each one. Can you help him? Read carefully and write the name where each animal belongs.

• Starting with the left, if you remove the basket where the CHICKEN was placed, only one basket will fall, the CHICK'S.

• If you remove the basket where the SHEEP was placed, the DUCK'S basket and the CHICK'S basket will fall.

• If you remove the basket where the BUNNY was placed, the CHICKEN'S basket and CHICK'S basket will fall.

• And if you remove the basket where the GOAT was placed, there will be a mess! Because the CHICKEN'S, the DUCK'S, and the CHICK'S basket will fall.

1) _____   4) _____

2) _____   5) _____

3) _____   6) _____

ON YOUR MARK, GET SET, GO...!

DIFFICULTY:
EASY ●
MEDIUM ○
HARD ○

25 The Correct Place

Place all the numbers that appear on the left on the diagram. They must all cross each other correctly vertically and horizontally. Two numbers have been placed to get you started.

12   698
16   785
34   5028
59   5316
81   8517
93   9468
~~498~~   ~~06868~~
684 425799

26 Rhyming Words

Link the words in the left column with those they rhyme with in the right column.

IMPROVE YOUR ENGLISH!

BOY	RAT
HAT	POLE
HOLE	BAKE
CAKE	TOY
BANK	TANK

Remember to write your answers on a separate sheet of paper!

27 Let's Outline ○

Without picking up your pen or going through the same line twice, try to draw the figure below. There are different solutions.

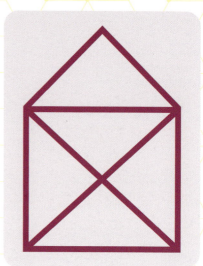

28 Order in the Kitchen ○

Look at the series shown here and choose the order that the items in the bottom row will be added.

 — — —  —

ON YOUR MARK, GET SET, GO...!

DIFFICULTY:
EASY ○
MEDIUM ○
HARD ○

29 Symbol Soup

There are five symbol sequences at the bottom of this page. Can you find them in the image below? Remember that these symbols must be in the same order (horizontally and vertically). Go for it, you can do it!

Answer Key...

1 Words with "Pet"
1. Carpet; 2. Petroleum; 3. Puppet; 4. Trumpet; 5. Petunia

2 Fifteen on Line
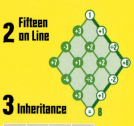

3 Inheritance

4 Pathway
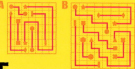

5 Doesn't Belong
Pair number 2. The purple color figure appears on the left unlike the rest where it is on the right.

6 Domino
The piece 2-3 is missing.

7 Trouble at the Farm
6 pigs, 7 rabbits, 1 chicken, 4 sheep.

8 The Key
The 3rd key is the correct one.

9 Alphabet Riddle
If you want something done right, do it yourself.

10 In Search of...

11 The Grove
There are 23 trees.

12 Girls' Names
1. MICHELLE; 2. KATHERINE; 3. TRACY; 4. MARY; 5. WENDY.

13 Weight
18 pounds. Why? Because each half of a brick weighs the same. If I say that a brick weighs "6 pounds more than half a brick" I would be saying that one half is 6 pounds. Therefore, three halfs (a brick and a half) add up to 18 pounds.

14 Distribution

15 Not Like the Others
The ball does not have eyes. The rest do.

16 What Letter Comes Next?
F, because each number is followed by the initial of its name.

17 More Vocabulary!
1. Cat; 2. Truck; 3. Library; 4. Colosseum.

18 Let's Remember!
1. Piano, bass, guitar
2. Clarinet, accordion, saxophone, trumpet, flute
3. There are 10 instruments.

19 Feelings Soup
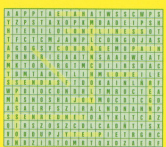

20 Planetary Sudoku

21 Crazy Maze

22 Continuing the Sequence
5, 2, 4

23 Movie Places
HOLLYWOOD
1. Ham; 2. Oil; 3. Lemon; 4. Lamp; 5. Yarn; 6. Owl; 7. Orange; 9. Duck

24 Inside the Baskets
1. Chick; 2. Chicken; 3. Duck; 4. Bunny; 5. Goat; 6. Sheep.

25 The Correct Place

26 Rhyming Words
BOY - TOY; HAT - RAT; HOLE - POLE; CAKE - BAKE; BANK - TANK

27 Let's Outline

28 Order in the Kitchen
The sequence follows alphabetical order, so the pepper mill is next, followed by the salt shaker, and finally, the scale.

29 Symbol Soup

24